I wish I were...

a pirate

Ivan Bulloch & Diane James

Created by Two-Can Publishing Ltd
346 Old Street
London EC1V 9NQ

Art Director Ivan Bulloch
Editor Diane James
Design Assistant Lisa Nutt
Illustrator Dom Mansell
Photographer Daniel Pangbourne
Models Kaz, Jonathan, Alicia,
Grant, Courtney, Abigail

This edition published 1997 by Two-Can Publishing Ltd

Paperback ISBN 1-85434-425-0
Hardback ISBN 1-85434-424-2

Dewey Decimal Classification 790.1

Printed in Spain by Graficromo S.A.

2 4 6 8 10 9 7 5 3

Contents

Pirates were fierce and brave sea robbers. They sailed the seas in search of merchant ships full of riches. After a bit of a battle the pirates tied up their prisoners and grabbed all the valuables on board. If you would like to be a pirate, you'll need to prepare before setting off on your adventures. *So let's begin...*

On the whole, pirates were a scruffy lot. They wore the same trousers and tops for days on end! Because they rushed around so much, their clothes soon got ragged and extremely smelly!

Pirates used scarves to keep their messy hair tied back and sometimes to stop their trousers falling down!

1 Fold a large scarf or square shape of material in half to make a triangle. Well done, that was the easy bit!

2 Hold one end in each hand and pull the long edge tight across your forehead. Take the ends round to the back and tie a knot.

3 For a different scarf, fold a square of material over and over to make a long strip. Wind it round your head and tie a knot.

4 To finish off your outfit, find an old T-shirt and cut a zig zag edge round the bottom. Tie some lengths of rope round the legs of your trousers.

7

Special pirates, like the Captain, wore a hat to show how brave and important they were. Very well-known pirates had their own scary badges which they wore proudly on their hats.

1 To make your own pirate's hat, measure your head with a tape measure. Use the measurement to cut out two shapes, like the ones below, from thick black paper. Glue them together at the sides.

glue   glue

Few pirates managed to escape getting injured in battle. That's why there were so many pirates with a black patch over one eye!

2 Cut some shapes from white paper to make a badge. You could make a scary skull and crossbones! Glue your badge pieces to the front of your hat.

3 Cut a shape like the one above from black paper to make your pirate's eye-patch. Make a hole at either side and thread through a length of cord. Tie the cord round your head.

No pirate felt safe without a weapon! They used swords and daggers for hand-to-hand fighting and guns for shooting. The captain made sure his crew sharpened and polished their tools every day until they sparkled!

Two swords are better than one!

1 Cut a sword or dagger shape from thick card. Corrugated card is best because it is thick, but not too difficult to cut.

2 Paint the blade and handle of your sword. If you wind some thick string round the handle it will give you a better grip.

Pirates needed to be able to see ships that were miles and miles away. A tiny spot on the horizon might be a ship full of riches – just perfect for a pirate raid! The best way to find out was by using a powerful telescope which made everything look very close.

Faster!

Ship Ahoy!
Look lively

1 Find two cardboard rolls. One should be small enough to fit inside the other. The small roll will be the eyepiece for your telescope and should be about half the length of the larger roll. Cut three strips from corrugated card to fit round the ends of the tubes.

2 Wind a card strip round each end of the long tube and one end of the short tube. Glue them down.

3 Push the smaller tube a short way into the longer one and paint all the pieces – black for the main parts and gold or yellow for the brass end pieces.

Pirate ships had to be strong and reliable. Huge sails helped speed them along. Life on board was pretty uncomfortable! There wasn't much room to move about, and it was often cold and damp!

1 Find a big, strong cardboard box. Cut off 3 of the flaps, leaving one short flap to make the prow. Shape it into a triangle.

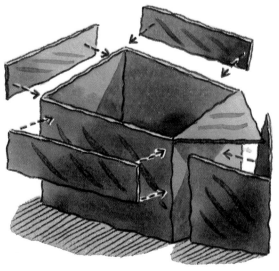

2 Glue the flaps to the sides and back of the box to look like planks. Cut a strip of card the same height as the box. Fold it in half and glue it to the prow and the sides.

The flag sailing from the top of the mast warned people off – a small red flag meant 'Prepare to Die'!

14

Look out, here I come!

3 Paint the background colour for your boat. Before it dries, paint on swirly stripes and rings to make the cardboard look like wood.

4 Use a sturdy tree branch for the mast – or an old broom handle. Cut a piece of material to the shape shown above and tie it to the end of the mast.

After a raid, pirates often had to find a safe place to hide their treasure. They had to make sure nobody could steal it before they could get back to retrieve it!

$\frac{1}{3}$

$\frac{2}{3}$

1 A large cardboard box makes a good treasure chest. Tape up the ends and cut round 3 sides – leaving one long side for the hinge.

2 Decorate your chest with coloured paper and chocolate coins. Don't forget a lock and key! Make holes in each of the short ends and poke some rope through to make handles. Now fill your chest with your favourite jewels.

The best place was in a strong, wooden chest with a lock. This was buried as deep as a pirate could possibly dig!

It was rare for a pirate to have a good memory. So, it was important to make a map to show where they had buried their treasure. It might be a very long time before they could get back to dig it up! The worst thing that could possibly happen was for the map to fall into enemy hands!

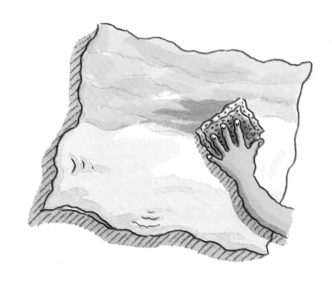

1 Take a sheet of plain white paper. Soak a teabag and squeeze out most of the water. Wipe it over the surface of the paper to make the paper look old.

Don't tell anyone else where the treasure is!

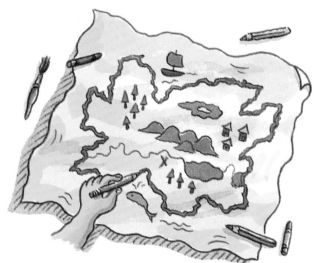

2 When the paper is dry, draw the outline of your map. Sketch on rivers, trees, and hills – anything that helps to pinpoint where the treasure is buried! Add a cross to mark the spot.

3 Crumple the map up to make it look even more old and wrinkled. Keep it in a secret place!

19

It wasn't often that you came across a healthy pirate! There were no vegetables or fresh fruit on board. For weeks on end pirates had to make do with salted food and dry biscuits.

Who's been nibbling my biscuit?

What little food they had was shared with the ships' rats and weevils – UGH!

20

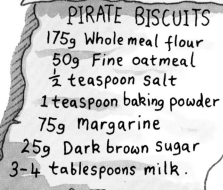

PIRATE BISCUITS
175g Wholemeal flour
50g Fine oatmeal
½ teaspoon salt
1 teaspoon baking powder
75g Margarine
25g Dark brown sugar
3-4 tablespoons milk.

1 Make your own pirate biscuits! Mix together the flour, oatmeal, salt, baking powder and sugar. Rub in the margarine until the mixture looks like breadcrumbs.

MILK

2 Pour the milk in and mix to a firm dough.

3 Put the dough on a floured surface and roll it out thinly. Use a small glass or cup, about 6cm wide, to cut out rounds.

4 Put the biscuits on a greased baking tray. Bake them in an oven set to 190°C (375°F, gas mark 5) for 15-20 minutes. When they are cool you can have a delicious pirate snack!

An attack by a pirate ship was a scary event! The pirates drew alongside and threw hooks and ropes over to keep the two ships together. Then they leapt aboard brandishing swords, daggers and pistols, making as much noise as possible! This was enough to make most people surrender immediately – before a single drop of blood was spilt.

A pirate's life was never, ever dull!

22

Pirates sometimes used words that would sound very strange nowadays! Here are just a few to help you carry on a pirate conversation. The words you would probably use today are underneath!

You lily-livered scaredy-cat

You're just a coward

Ahoy there me hearties!

Hi, how are you?

Seize my soul if I give you quarter

You're not getting anything from me

Scurvy knave!

Spotty face!

Shiver me timbers!

What a surprise!